The Dog Lovers' Guide to the Good Life

By Carol Saxe and Hanita Blumfield
Artwork by Carol Saxe

ISBN   978-0-615-17560-7

Published by Pawsome Press
New York City & East Hampton, New York

Saxe Studio
www.saxestudio.com; saxestudio@optonline.net

Hanita Blumfield
hblumfield@nyc.rr.com

Dedications

For my mother,
Marjorie Mayers Saxe,
who taught me to love and respect animals
and
to honor all of the amazing animals that
have shared my life and home;
Chou Chou, Puff, Hamlet, Hampton,
Cindy, Taxi, Aspen and Vail.

Carol Saxe

This book is dedicated with love and remembrance:
To my mother and sister who encouraged me to value beauty in all creatures, especially animals whose soul
shines through eyes that see the world without guile;
To my husband whose music speaks the universal language of love and compassion and whose gifts bring great
joy and especially;
To Zoë- companion, guide, muse and angel on earth who surely is now at one with the universe and whose
memory will live in our hearts forever
and
To all the other animals who are seeking their "forever home"- may they know compassion, love and joy.

Dr. Hanita Blumfield

Contents

Preface

Shortly after moving to East Hampton with my husband and our two terriers, I began a series of paintings depicting dogs on the beach; just dogs, with no people. The paintings were quite different from the architectural paintings of New York and Paris that I had been working on for several years and which had brought me some success.

These paintings were inspired by the canine social scene at our local beaches and depicted the dogs pretty much as they are or as I envision they aspire to be; playing, swimming, socializing and sunning themselves. Soon the "dog paintings" had become the most popular and successful work I had ever done as a painter. Having volunteered with animal rescue groups for quite a few years, I was thrilled to have found a way to combine my passion for painting with my love of animals.

With my children grown and out of the house, I had more time to spend with my canine companions and from there things pretty much continued to go to the dogs! The dog art subject matter expanded to the city and beyond. Opportunities presented themselves and a whole new world of dogdom emerged.

A dear friend, Jeff Silberman, suggested I write a guide for people looking for interesting places to go with their dogs. A quick perusal of web sites revealed many listings of dog parks and pet friendly hotels all over the country.. The Dog Lover's Guide to the Good Life evolved as a hybrid. The guide attempts to make the readers aware of the most interesting, unusual, fun activities and places for people and their dogs. The guide is meant as an "eye opener" to the types of venues that exist and how to find these venues where you live or travel. We hope that the canine contribution will provide a voice for your dog as you chose potential activities to participate in and places to visit.

On a more serious note, we truly value our canine companions. We urge all dog lovers to think first of adoption and rescue. I will continue to work towards the humane treatment of all dogs and cats, the end of euthanasia of healthy and young animals, the end of puppy mills, and an end to the suffering of animals used in medical laboratories.

Carol Saxe Buda

I had just completed a book on the memoirs of a woman who survived the Holocaust in Europe. She was saved by ten British prisoners of war who risked their lives to help a 15-year-old girl escape the Nazi death march. This was an emotional book for me to write as it dealt with both the worst that humans inflict on each other and the best that fortitude and courage exemplify.

I was ready for a change and when Carol Saxe asked me to collaborate on a book about the Good Life for Dogs, I welcomed the opportunity to write about the strong bond between canines and their human companions.

Dogs are our companions. Loving us in spite of our faults and ecstatic when they share our activities. They have become, for many, anchors in an uncertain world and soul mates as we journey through life. As Roger Caras stated, "Dogs are not our whole life, but they make our lives whole."

Because of the extraordinary bond between us, we have a duty to protect our canine companions from the cruelty that some callous and downright evil individuals have inflicted on helpless animals. Puppy mills must be stopped. Shelters that kill healthy animals because they are too crowded must be given the resources to expand adoption programs. And most of all the public needs to be educated about how to value and care for a species that may not speak in words, but speaks from the heart with deeds of undying devotion and love.

We hope you enjoy this book as we had a wonderful time visiting and reviewing (actually our dogs did the reviewing) some fabulous places to take your best friend,

Dr. Hanita Blumfield

The Dog Lovers' Guide to the Good Life

Written by Carol Saxe and Hanita Blumfield
Artwork by Carol Saxe

During the last one hundred years, the role of dogs in human society has changed dramatically. For centuries before the industrial revolution, most dogs had important jobs; assisting their humans with farming, herding, hunting, tracking and protection. Dogs herded sheep, protected livestock, kept rats out of feed and fended off predators. Before the arrival of the modern day automobile, dogs could freely and safely roam their farms and small towns.

Unfortunately, for many dogs today their lives involve long hours alone at home waiting for their human companions to return from work or the many places they go where DOGS ARE NOT ALLOWED.

Today there are more than 61 million dogs in the United States and people spend over $31 billion in caring for their canine companions. The ties that bind are not merely commercial but are the result of the love and affection that exists between the two species. Dogs help us alleviate the stress of an uncertain and increasingly complex world. A growing array of services and venues is being offered to dog lovers who truly care for and value their beloved dogs and want to do the best for them.

The Dog Lovers' Guide to the Good Life attempts to introduce people to some of the unusual opportunities that exist for people and dogs to experience together, as well as places and people who strive to meet your dog's needs for play, socialization, and companionship. Since people love to be with their canine companions as much as dogs want to be with their special people, we have searched for venues that welcome your dog as a member of the family. For dog lovers togetherness is truly the good life.

We have two teams of dogs and their companions willing and eager to check out the "good life". Our dogs will relate their canine experience to help you understand the four legged perspective. The dogs have all agreed to sniff out special places and activities that will have appeal to a diverse group of furry friends. They will use the bark system with the highest accolade being five barks and one bark signifying - don't go!

Dogs are pack animals who love and need to be with their humans companions. Dogs communicate to their special family how much they want to be with them. They express deep sadness and concern when their humans leave and great joy when they come back. Some dogs will bring their leash to the door. One dog, Raider, even carried his Loews Loves pets bowl around the house while his lady packed. That was clever!

The group is going to check out the W hotel in New York City. The W hotels have a fabulous Woof / Meow "Paws are Welcome" program, which not only allows dogs to stay with their families but also works hard to make their visit memorable.

Our four canine reviewers have different personalities and needs. We hope they will aid the reader in evaluating these venues for their own dogs.

 Aspen is an adorable terrier mix with a lot of Jack Russell in her genes; an exceedingly bright, adventurous thirty pound alpha dog. Brave and social, she chose her companion, Vail, for his good looks and submissive qualities.

 Vail is a bit smaller and quite handsome. He is generally nervous around dogs he doesn't know, but is otherwise a sweet, affectionate fellow who loves treats.

 Zoe is a beautiful silky haired toy Yorkie who has known only love and affection since she was a small one pound pup. She expects care and comfort wherever she goes and rarely walks when she can be carried. She taught Mazel, who became her fearless friend, what canine bonding is all about.

 Mazel is a fearless 4 pound Yorkie whose mission in life is to protect his family and friends. Each day is an adventure that he meets with zest. Zoe thinks that he is as handsome as he is brave and never worries about larger dogs when he is by her side.

Look for their informative reviews as we visit different venues. The number of barks each dog gives will be the key!

The Dogs Take a Bite out of the Big Apple

A VISIT TO THE W HOTEL

A growing number of hotels around the country not only accept dogs, but also welcome them. Increasingly, people traveling with canine companions have a wide choice of accommodations including some that are both elegant and sophisticated. In New York City, the W Hotels, the St. Regis, the Tribeca Grand and the Soho Grand are some of the hotels that welcome dogs. The Loews Hotels have a "Loews Loves Pets" program. We will visit the W Hotel in New York and the Loews Coronado Bay Hotel in San Diego, California as well as some special inns in Vermont and a beautiful resort in Florida.

 Set in the bustling area of Union Square, the W Hotel attracts a hip and trendy crowd. The bar area at the W boasts wonderful window seats designed to view the New York scene.

The hotel is an imposing structure, complete with gargoyles. The Doorman smiles at the dogs and ushers them in. It is a new experience for one of the companions who often had to hide Mazel and Zoë as the welcome in other places was less than friendly and she would not leave them behind. The concierge stops to pet each dog and comments on how beautiful they are.   More important to our canine pals, he dispenses treats and gifts. For a few minutes, the dogs revel in being the center of attention. There is a doggie bowl with woof written on the bottom, which is really cute. He assures us that the rooms are equipped with comfortable dog beds as well as terry cloth robes similar to the ones for us. In addition, we are given a book which lists 101 interesting places to go with the dogs in New York City.   Dog walking can be arranged, if necessary.

Ratings for the W Hotel

Very comfortable and welcoming, but I have to admit that I was very uncomfortable and uncharacteristically scared in the elevator

Silly robe but terrific food, friendly people!

Fun toys and room to play

Sublime bed and great atmosphere!

The Dog Park

The dog park in Union Square is one of many in New York City, of which a complete list can be found at the end of the book. For suburban or country dogs staying at the hotel unused to the crowds and hubbub of the city sidewalks, a trip to the dog park in Union Square is a necessity.

We chose to visit a larger, prettier park with river views.   Peter Detmold Park, located at 49th Street and 1st Avenue, is a small slice of dog heaven. The park is part of a tree lined, flower laden oasis, facing the East River. The fenced dog run, two blocks long, is a safe place for urban canines to run and play. The dogs are well socialized and mix well with one another. All sizes and shapes of dogs were there when we visited. A playground is adjacent to the dog park. Both children and dogs romp in this lovely, riverside setting, somewhat removed from the traffic, hustle and bustle of the city.

Ratings for the Dog Park

 *Interesting experience. I did like the German Shepherd.*

 Too many strange, scary dogs. Not my comfort zone at all!

 I am too short! This wasn't the "big easy" it was the "big pushy".

 I would rather watch Animal Planet in the hotel.

Saks Fifth Avenue

The dogs are finally going to Zoë's territory, Saks Fifth Avenue. The department store is on one of the most beautiful avenues in the world, Fifth Avenue, across from Rockefeller Center and the ice skating rink. Zoë wants to check out the new dog line of clothes designed by Paige and Gail – it's called Juicy Couture and it seems good enough to eat.

The dogs are all greeted and petted and one woman really wants take Zoë home. No way! They make their way to the 8th floor and the dogs are really having fun with everyone making a big fuss over them. There is a group of dog companions who are sitting in a circle, admiring the dog beds, sweaters and leather leashes. Dog coats in a variety of colors are very popular as well. The women are sharing dog stories and hints about how to teach the dogs etiquette so that they will be welcomed at the stores and many of the tourist sites in the city.

Stores welcome well-behaved dogs on a leash or, for the designer dogs, being carried in a variety of pet carriers. New York dogs are highly sociable because they enter establishments where there are crowds, noise and often the sounds of music. The places where dogs are not welcomed are food establishments, and even that ban is circumvented by permitting animals to stay with their companions at outdoor cafes and designated dog establishments where humans are allowed to enter.

Ratings

I need a valet and a big dog to make a path for me!

The coat makes me proud.

Restaurants NYC

After the shopping spree at Saks Fifth Avenue and a look at the ice skaters at Rockefeller Center, the group decides to visit a special restaurant called **Fetch** located at 1649 3rd Avenue.

Fetch is a wonderful example of an establishment that not only welcomes animals but also is devoted to them. The outdoor café is only one of the signs of their loyalty to dogs. There is a wall that is hung with framed pictures of dog patrons and their friends. Another wall has pictures of dogs waiting to be adopted as fetch works with Animal Haven to find good homes for dogs without families.

Another example is **The Barking Dog** restaurant on 34th Street between Third and Lexington. There is a large bricked patio on the side of the restaurant, peacefully set back from the street where patrons are encouraged to dine with their canine companions. People can enjoy a beautiful selection of dog themed art on the walls and order drinks such as a Chihuahua, a Sit Stay or a Maine Coonhound. The Barking Dog has an annual canine costume party with prizes and fun for all. If your dog is very social and doesn't mind being dressed up, this is a good opportunity to get out together and mix, mingle and make some new friends.

Ratings

This is kind of boring just sitting here on the sidewalk watching them eat. I feel like a tag along.

Oh, it's not that bad...better than sitting at home by ourselves; and where there is food, there are sure to be leftovers!

It's nice to be where the big dogs won't step on me.

I like the idea of my picture on the wall.

Central Park

Central Park is a magnificent oasis of green delight in the midst of the most" built" city in the world. There are paths and walkways through woods and fields. Beautiful historic structures and plazas dot the park and magnificent plantings adorn the park in the spring. Leash laws are strictly observed between 9 am and 9 pm. People who want their dogs to run and play off leash enter the park in the morning and congregate in such places as "dog hill" You won't find it on a map, but if one walks northwest from the Hans Christian Anderson Statue beyond the toy boat pond you may see a hill where small dogs and their companions have congregated. The Central Park dog guide is a downloadable guide provided by the conservancy and can be accessed from the Central Park site.

 Our furry friends enter the Park at East 79th street and walk toward the toy boat lagoon. The area is full of children happily steering the miniature boats and people reading the New York Times at tables located at the outdoor café. Our foursome is not particularly hungry as Fetch had a good assortment of favorite foods but they watch as the boats race across the water.

Central Park Ratings

Not allowed to be off the leash- but this is the best place in the city.

The leash pulled on my collar and made me cough. I couldn't chase squirrels. But I would love to come back early in the morning when I can run off leash.

I don't have time to enjoy the scenery. I have to take four steps to each one you guys take just to keep up. I'm exhausted. I need to soothe my aching paws.

Being carried is nice- I can see everything.

The Dog Run

Well, the dogs are in luck because it's Saturday in New York and there is a recreational swim hour at The Dog Run pool. The Dog Run is located at 136 Ninth Avenue in Chelsea. A multi-service canine facility, The Dog Run has the only heated pool for dogs in all five boroughs in addition to fully supervised active daycare, training, grooming and yes, even swimming lessons! Check them out online at www.thedogrun-nyc.com. We decide to check them out in person. On Saturday from three to four and on Sunday from two to three they have free swim time open to the public. The small pool is inviting with a wall of glass that looks out on a lovely little garden. They accommodate on average about five dogs and their owners, who can join their dogs in the pool if they want or just toss toys for them to fetch. Mazel wants to soak his aching paws and Aspen just wants to have fun. Vail and Zoë are skeptical, but might get their feet wet.

Aspen is delighted to leap into the water after her ball. Mazel soaks his paws on the first step. Zoë and Vail are happy to watch for a while until Zoë suggests that they leave and go the Soho Grand Bar and Lounge to get some treats without having to work for them.

The Soho Grand Bar and Lounge is in the Soho Grand Hotel at 310 West Broadway. The lounge welcomes the canine crowd and if they decide to spend the night the rooms have dog pillows. Pedicures are available for pampered pooches!

Ratings for the Dog Run recreational swim

   *I could do this for hours.*

I was nervous that I would get pushed in the pool.

   No, thank you!

   *Lovely warm water, but I got splashed in the face.*

Agility at ARF is an Art

Agility courses are found throughout the country. Pet training facilities, pet organizations, and community education centers may offer courses. Humans and animals find satisfaction in working as teams to conquer the course and to have lots of fun in the process. So agility is fun for dogs and fun for people! Some people and their dogs go on to advanced classes and some make a serious hobby out of agility and go on to compete in timed events. At the competition level there is great exercise for all.

The agility course that we attended is set up in a fenced area of the Animal Rescue Fund, our local animal rescue organization. There are hurdles to jump, tunnels to whiz through, hoops to go through, poles to sidestep, a ramp to climb and a broad jump. Aspen and Vail have signed up for agility. Mazel and Zoë have respectfully declined. Our classmates are a Dobie, a Great Dane, a German Shorthair Pointer and a Dachshund.

Aspen meets and greets each dog with ease. Vail seemed a bit more tentative and thankfully, the big dogs seemed well behaved and weren't really bothering him.
As soon as the instructor and people participants brought out the treats, the dogs were eagerly attentive and anxious to do something, ANYTHING, to get their treats. They followed the treats through the course accepting their rewards along the way. Aspen had some difficulty with the weave poles. Vail was very apprehensive about going over the top of the steep ramp. He needed lots of encouragement to launch into the unknown the first time. Both dogs excelled through the rest of the course, soon anxious to repeat the tasks for more treats.

Their terrier genes were on display as they were the only dogs in the class who could go through a long, looped tunnel with ease. We all watched the Great Dane who was terribly uneasy about the tunnel even though his companion was on her hands and knees giving a demonstration!

Ratings for Agility

I wish I had started when I was much younger. I could have been competitive at this!

The wooden mountain was scary to go up and over, but the rest was easy. The treats were excellent and, hey, I'll do anything within reason for food.

Loews Loves Pets

Loews Hotels provides memorable vacations for families and their pets. We have chosen to profile three of their most innovative programs "Su'ruff Camp" at the Loews Coronado Bay Resort, "The Hounds of Music" at the Loews Vanderbilt Hotel Nashville, and the "Outward Hound' at Loews Denver Hotel As Jonathan Tisch said," Children and even their parents have long enjoyed the learning opportunities that travel affords, whether learning to kayak, mastering yoga or simply exploring new surroundings. Now the beloved family pet.... can be an integral part of it." Hotels take on a new breed of clients who want to travel with their animals (Kathleen Cochran, General Manager)

We received an email from our friend Raider and his companions. They went to the Loew's in Coronado Beach and Raider learned to surf. He was even on TV and got to go back for the annual Surf Dog Competition. He didn't wear his surfing shorts gift from the Hotel, but he did wear his surfer bandana. He really caught the wave and had an awesome time. He told us he could go anywhere in the hotel except for the pool- even to the piano bar – but they didn't want him to sing. There was even a Gondola ride, enjoyed by all.

After settling into their very comfortable rooms, the dogs head out to Dog Beach [yes, that's really the name] to meet their surf instructor who is delighted to meet them. Vail cools his feet in the shallow water and then hangs back hoping the instructor won't notice him. He has no intention of getting wet. Zoë goes off to sunbathe on a towel. Mazel has decided to withhold judgment and watch for a while.

Aspen, however, is all ears and wiggles, excited to play with her new friend. The instructor and her special person head out into the splashing water with their big toy, which magically floats on top of the water. Aspen follows her family into the water to be near them and make sure they get back to shore. Once beyond the foaming water, the instructor lifts Aspen onto the magic board. They push the board forward, it wobbles a bit and Aspen jumps off to be with her special person. They lift Aspen onto the board again and this time she stands cautiously, feet spread, while the board reaches the beach. She seems to "get it" and when they go out again and lift Aspen onto the board, she stands confidently and rides the board in to shore. Everyone is beside themselves with excitement at her new found skill. Aspen is the center of all this positive attention and enjoying every minute of it!

After rolling in the sand to dry off and a few good shakes, it's time for the dogs and their companions to go back to the Hotel. A fabulous surf n turf dinner arrives at the room for the dogs. This place is absolutely magical! . This really is the good life!

Meanwhile, Mazel and Zoë go off with their companion to visit the doggie spa. They take turns having pawdicures and massage. So much to do here and so little time!

Loews Su'rff Dog Ratings

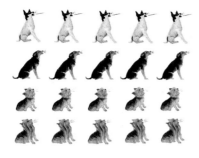

The surfing is awesome!

Love the hotel- the room, the food, the people and being with my family. Just please don't make me get wet.

The piano bar reminds me of home; loved the mall – so many toys!

The Gondola Ride – I felt as if I were being serenaded in Italy

Hound of Music at the Loews Nashville Vanderbilt Hotel

It is another doggie email. This one from Cotton and Powder, gorgeous Bichons who told us they had a wonderful time at the Nashville Vanderbilt Hotel.

This sounds really great, so we are off on our next adventure! This time it's a cultural affair with a big C. We are going to cut a record.

The program is called Hound of Music. Canines and their companions share a plush room with room service for pets, a grooming session, massage and then the special event; a limo ride to the studio and the creation of a personalized CD. At the studio, the dogs are set up with mikes and headsets. Their vocalizations are recorded digitally, then professionally mixed and arranged onto a disc. After some noise, some fun, some treats and a wonderful CD, the dogs are truly Hounds of Music. Fame can't be far behind!

Ratings for Hound of Music

I am a star!

I don't like being a backup.

The next CD is mine!

I was bored.

Outward Hound at the Loews Denver Hotel

At the Loews Denver Hotel, dogs receive the same warm welcome and a variety of canine amenities. Our Outward Hound package included water and food bowls, a mat, dog treat, and collapsible pet travel dish and water carrier. Their human companions receive maps of pet friendly trails, parks and other venues.

Personal pet hikes which include two hours of off leash fun and supervised swim time are also available with limo pick up and drop off included! A company called Adventure Hounds will come and pick up your dog and transport your furry friend along with a few other dogs to their several acre lakeside property for supervised play. Sorry, this activity is for dogs only. The company runs one trip to their dog park in the morning and one in the afternoon. The dogs are harnessed into seats or otherwise separated for the limo ride. If you have a social dog who won't mind leaving you behind, the adventure park may be an option to pursue.

Ratings for Outward Hound :

Fun, fun, fun... after the car ride!

Great place, but I had to be nice to a lot of new dogs that I didn't know.

Camp Gone to the Dogs

Going to camp with your dog is an excellent way to experience and explore new activities with your pup. Dog camps are also a great way to train a new dog, to bond and to meet other dog lovers as crazy as yourself. We chose one of the best-known camps. Camp Gone to the Dogs in Vermont. There are other camps located in various parts of the country. A list is provided in our information index. Camps typically run for a week, some only for a weekend.

Camp Gone to the Dogs offers a session in the spring and two one-week sessions during fall foliage season. For the Fall camp, they provide an all inclusive price with room and board at a lovely inn in Stowe or you can chose your own accommodations and attend the daily camp activities. The camp brings highly qualified trainers from around the country to offer an amazing array of activities. You can choose several activities ranging from really reliable recall to agility, flyball, herding, tracking, clicker training, dock diving and the like. Lectures and discussions fill in the evenings and, of course, there is some free time for hiking and enjoying the countryside with your dog.

The camp has classes for beginners and for those more advanced. If you have ever watched dogs competing on animal planet and thought that could be you, camp is the way to go. Competing with one's dog is a growing hobby. Your dog may have talents that you can't even imagine. Dog camp is one way to find out!

Dock Diving

Aspen has been signed up for Dock Diving class and heads down to the pond with her companion. You may have seen a dock diving competition on Animal Planet. The dogs take a running leap off a dock chasing a kong, ball or favorite toy. The distance they cover before hitting the water is measured. Some dogs are naturals for this activity and readily leap off the dock. Others need incremental encouragement. The fun of chasing the ball and swimming are inherently rewarding for these dogs. The praise and attention just add to the fun!

Aspen seemed intent on hitting the water without getting her ears wet and worked hard at perfecting her dry ear technique. Vail, who dislikes being wet above his elbows, watched apprehensively from what he felt was a safe distance away. Unbeknownst to him, he would soon be on his way to Tracking class.

Ratings for Dock Diving

 *Fun! Fun! Fun!*

 Can you give negative barks for death defying leaps into deep water? I have to go hide from this activity.

Tracking

At Camp Gone to the Dogs, tracking is a popular class. Before the class begins four flags are placed out on a large field to mark a course for the human part of the team and four items, socks or gloves, are hidden along the way with treats inside. After 45 minutes the scent has intensified and settled so that the tracking can begin! Vail has left the death defying leaps into deep water to Aspen and friends, and has signed up for tracking class with his companion. They arrive at a large field where an array of interesting scents abounds.

A special tracking harness with a long leash attached is placed on each dog. The human part of the team announces "track" and they head toward the first pungent sock. At this point the dog is given a high reward treat and lots of praise. "Track" is announced again and this time the dogs are already on the scent. Vail had received a piece of chicken. He is all over the scent and soon arrives at the next sock. Another treat! Vail is off in a hurry towards the next scent. By the time Vail reaches the fourth and final treat he is wagging his tail and eagerly looking to do it again.

After a few sessions, the dogs will associate the harness with the tracking activity. At that point, just donning the harness will make most dogs excited as they anticipate the tracking activity. They love to "work" at this natural task.

Vail returned home from camp with a useful skill. He assisted my neighbor in looking for her lost cat. We were all so proud!

Rating for Tracking:

 *This was great! I really found my "inner dog" here.*

41

While at camp, Aspen excelled at retrieving and went wild at flyball. Aspen and Vail were a bit out of control at herding class.

Zoe attended Freestyle Dancing with her companion. Freestyle dancing requires a human to partner with a dog to dance together. It was hard to tell who was having more fun! Zoe twirled, swirled and jumped around her partner with poise and passion. They may even have a future in competition.

As for Mazel he went to retrieving class where he proudly retrieved his neon pink barbells.

Camp Ratings

Wow! Herding was really exciting.

Ditto!

Retrieving was fun, but I was worried that a big dog would come and take my favorite toy which I do not share!

Freestyle Dancing. This is my passion!

Vermont
Inn at Quail Run

Aspen and Vail have arrived in Wilmington, Vermont near Mt. Snow with their family, who unbeknownst to them, plan to do some skiing. The first stop will be at the Inn at Quail Run where Victoria Lawhorne, the Inn's owner, is expecting them. The dogs meet and greet the owner's four children and four dogs. There is plenty of room to romp in the snow and even a fenced area where they can hang out and play.

At the Inn at Quail Run, the dogs stay in your room with you. Well behaved, social dogs need not be confined and can enjoy the amenities of the Inn with their human companions. For a reasonable fee, the owner's children will dog sit your four legged friend while you ski , shop or dine out. Their friendly service includes lots of play time and affection!

Vermont is a great place to visit with your dog any time of year, but particularly in the warmer months. Many of the activities, such as hiking, swimming, kayaking etc, can be enjoyed with your dog.

Ratings for Inn at Quail Run:

I would have given these 5 barks if my people had not left me so much. If we returned to the Inn, I would be used to it and I would give it 5 barks.

The people were very nice and were very affectionate to me. The Inn was warm and the food was good too.

Paw House Inn

Our group continued north to the Paw House Inn in West Rutland near the Killington ski area. The Paw House is more than dog friendly; they cater to dog lovers and their dogs. Before you arrive, they ask you to fill out a dog profile so they will be better able to accommodate your dog's needs. They have an onsite training center which offers agility and obedience training sessions that you can arrange to attend. Or perhaps you prefer a Canine Mystery Weekend to have a "terrierizing experience".

During the summer the Paw House has a dog-in theatre where you can watch a movie with your canine companion outside in the yard. There are many activities dogs and their humans can enjoy together including hiking, swimming and the like. There are also lots of activities and restaurants which might require leaving your four legged love behind.

Dogs stay in the room with you when you are at the Inn with their own comfy beds. However, they do not stay in the rooms when their human companions go out without them, as the owners feel that the dogs are more stressed left in the rooms alone. The Paw House Inn provides Mario's Playhouse 24/7 to accommodate your dog if you need to leave him behind. Visitors may use this facility on a self-serve basis. During the day the innkeeping staff will come and walk, hike, feed or play with the dogs. The Inn is planning a recreation center which will house indoor agility and obedience training and hopefully a vet clinic as well.

Unlike the Inn at Quail Run, the dogs are not hanging out in the kitchen or tagging along with children when you are gone, however, many dogs are quite used to crating or some kind of kennel situation and are quite content in Mario's Playhouse while their humans are out. The Paw House Inn is a great place to visit in the warmer months as most of their activities are geared to dogs and their human companions.

Ratings for the Paw House Inn:

I had some serious fun here. I do get uncomfortable being left in strange places. If I came back I would be used to it and then I would give 5 barks.

I wasn't worried. I knew they were coming back. Anyway, I wasn't alone, I was with Aspen.

Florida

THE RITZ CARLTON

Sarasota, Florida has a number of accommodations for the canine that accompanies the family to this vacation paradise. The Ritz-Carlton invites dogs and cats who weigh 20 pounds or less to enjoy the luxury of this world class hotel. Rover may need to go on a pre-vacation diet! There are special welcome amenities, designated dog-walking areas on the property and a dog and cat bakery shop. Canines are welcome on the shuttle to shop at the famous St. Armand's designer area.

Since Aspen and Vail, who each weigh in about 10 pounds over the limit, can't go to the Ritz, Mazel and Zoe won't go either. Sometimes it pays to be small but you can't abandon your friends.

TURTLE BEACH HOTEL, located at 9049 Midnight Pass Road, Siesta Key is a dog lover's paradise.

Situated on the shores of Little Sarasota Bay, the Turtle Beach Hotel is recognized with a five-paw rating from Florida Dog Lovers Companion. Dogs are welcome to stay in the cottages (two per cottage) and to run on a dog-friendly beach a few miles south of the resort. Your canine companions are allowed to be in the hotel's kayaks, canoes and paddleboats. They are welcome in the village and the shopkeepers make sure that there is food and water for them.

The cottages are very private and each has its own private, outdoor space. Our group makes its way down to the "dog beach" where the dogs are allowed to run free and explore. As the tide recedes, small sandy islands emerge and we can walk, swim or kayak out to them. Birds are everywhere. Vail is happily and haplessly pursuing them while Aspen is digging in the sand and Mazel and Zoe watch from their beach towel.

Turtle Beach Hotel Ratings

My kind of place – lots to do- swim, dig sand, explore....

I loved the privacy.

Great Kayak ride!

The swim to the doggie island was my exercise for the year.

Yappy Hour

Parties with dogs and their special people have become very popular. They are occasions for dog lovers to get together, admire the dogs and share stories. In a time when dogs often are treated as children, advice is given and much affection and love is shared. The dog parties can be fundraisers, get togethers, birthday parties and even a new experience called yappy hour – where canines and their companions share several hours of socializing. We attended several.

New York Dog Magazine hosted a Black Tie for Dogs party at a Dog Themed Art Gallery in Chelsea, which raised funds for The Mayors Alliance for NYC animals. The event was crowded and I feel confident that Aspen and Vail will tell you that it was more fun for the people than for the dogs, but they were good sports about their costumes. Zoë and Mazel, however, were perfectly happy being carried around the room getting lots of eye level attention. They all enjoyed gourmet cookies.

If you would like to attend a dog party in your area, check with local canine boutiques, animal rescue groups, magazines and newspapers, or organize a party to benefit a charity, or just for fun.

New York Dog Magazine throws a party at the W Hotel

It's a party! Bring your dogs.

The Ballroom of the W is set up with drinks for the humans including white and red wine and tablecloths festively arranged, There are treats, cookies and cakes made for dogs but fit for human consumption- delicious! Vendors have come to display the latest in canine couture and travel luggage. The material is of the finest quality including velvets, tartans and soft cashmere. Luxe beds are also on display.

Ringing the room are fabulous dog portraits and places to meet the artists. People greet each other and share the latest achievements of their beloved dogs. A small black Chihuahua sporting a jeweled collar wags her minute tail at a Golden Retriever dressed in a red bandana. A woman walks by with two Maltese in a baby carriage- they are much older but still enjoy the party. The carob treats and Doggie cakes are a big hit and some of the humans are seen munching along.

Towards the end of the party a group of women with Chihuahuas form a circle on the floor to share stories and helpful hints about the care of these tiny but sturdy dogs that are the favorites of the moment. Our dogs carefully maneuver through the crowded room. Aspen is always eager to greet new dogs. Vail would much prefer a quiet corner. After eating through their goody bags, the party is pretty much over for the four legged set, while their human companions finish their wine and conversation!

Party Rating

 *The party was a little boring, but I do like to be included.*

 *Too crowded for me. The treats were the highlight.*

 I was almost RUN OVER!

 *Nice. I always like a good party...see and be seen...you know*

Summer Dog Party in the Hamptons

The various shades of green are fit for an artist's palette and the rolling hills are an enticement for dogs to gambol and play. Acres and Acres of verdant lawns and graceful old shade trees encompass this stunningly beautiful East Hampton estate. Our Gracious hosts are giving this party to celebrate the release of the new Animal Rescue Fund Calendar and dogs and their companions are invited for cocktails and finger foods. There are platters of shrimp sharing space with doggie biscuits and lots of cool drinks for animals and humans.

This property has an infinity pool where one edge becomes a waterfall and the dogs are very intrigued by where the water is going. One large Newfoundland braves the edge and swims in the pool. One curious dachshund falls in by mistake and is quickly plucked from the water. Vail and Aspen both decide that the shape of this water is strange to them and they are steering clear. An Italian Greyhound makes friends with Mazel. But if they decide to run, Mazel clearly has no way of keeping up.

So many breeds are represented from Pit Bulls, Poodles, Westies and Bichons to Shepherds and wonderful glorious mixed breeds who bring their fascinating beauty to the party. Soon the dogs are off leash and wandering off to make new friends and play while their companions keep a watchful eye. Everyone is well behaved and having a marvelous time.

Ratings for Dog Party:

I belonged there. I don't understand why I haven't been invited to a party like this before!

I wish I had Aspen's confidence in crowds.

What's not to like?

I had fun!

Tails of The Beach

The beaches of East Hampton are among the most beautiful in the world with miles of pristine sand and the special light that artists and writers who have lived here have made famous. Although there are many dog lovers in the Hamptons, there are restrictions as to when and where dogs may come and frolic in the sand and surf. The Village of East Hampton has different rules for dogs on the beach than the Town of East Hampton. The village bans dogs during the day, whereas the Town allows dogs in certain areas anytime.

Many communities ban dogs during the day; some for the entire summer season. County and State rules can also vary and postings may be vague. Passersby can be just plain wrong. Check with a knowledgeable source concerning beaches you wish to visit for accurate information. Internet guides are available for many areas and offer updated info. **Be sure to pick up after your pet**! Having our dogs at the beach to swim and play is a privilege that we want to protect.

One of the most popular morning gathering spots in the Village of East Hampton is Wyborg Beach. There are other beaches where dogs can go at any time of day, but the morning gathering is very popular in the summer. A core group of regulars cruise the beach between eight and nine with coffee and their dogs. Both the dogs and people have formed friendships and social bonds. The more adventurous water loving dogs chase their balls out into the surf. A good time is had by all.

Another group of people and dogs frequents Main Beach at 6 pm. The ocean sparkles with white-capped waves and looks gray blue in the twilight. The sand is a fine powder and families are beginning to search for missing toy shovels, rainbow colored towels and sand trucks that have done duty as they have transported children to the places that dreams are made of. . The heat of the day has given way to a cool comfortable breeze from the water. Dogs have joined their families playing ball and swimming in the surf.

Ratings for the beach:

I love the beach, digging in the sand and especially fetching balls out of the water.

I Love running free and chasing birds.

Maybe the Chihuahua will become a good friend.

Nah. I don't really like the sand.

The Barking Hills Country Club

The Barking Hills Country club in New Jersey not only has weekend camps with activities such as flyball, agility and lure coursing; they also supply dogs for television, commercials and film! It's definitely time to get Rover off the couch. So let's follow Aspen, Vail and the other canine kids to camp and read their review.

We have chosen to profile Barking Hills Country Club because of the variety of activities it offers and the camp's recognition that dogs, like their human companions, have different abilities and needs. Learning, working and playing helps create a good canine "citizen" who is a joy to be with and who may work in diverse settings such as hospitals, search and rescue, physical, recreational and psychological therapy and yes, even, performing on the runway during Fashion Week.

There are a number of facets to its mission that include a weekend camp with activities such as flyball, agility, lure coursing, and learning tricks. Barking Hills understands that size matters and has an agility course that is miniaturized for small dogs. Other programs include puppy beginning and kindergarten classes, dog obedience as well as specialized training to be therapy dogs and at the other end of the spectrum, learning to be entertainers in commercials.

In the winter months Barking Hills holds a once a week game night, where you can come with your canine companions to socialize and have fun. There are even dogs that bowl and get together as a team- although some have been known to cheat by running down the lane and pushing the pins with their paws to get a strike,

The Not for Profit "Dogs in Service" trains and supervises animal assisted therapy and is goal oriented, supervised by professionals and well documented. The dog often acts as an intermediary whether it is helping a person with a physical handicap or having a child explain why the dog won't take its medicine (needs apple juice). In effect communication moves through the trained canine because people may be uncomfortable when speaking about themselves

Barking Hills has an interesting program that helps fund its not for profit work. "Lights, Camera, Action" classes train dogs for commercials and other entertainment work. Canines have appeared on Saturday Night Live, One Life to Live and commercials for Target, American Express, Lowes, Home Depot and fashion runway work. All types of dogs have been featured including Cocker Spaniels, Labradoodles, and Terrier Mixes. The requirements to be successful include being cute, being able to work with noise, learning how to bark or eliminate on command, and at a minimum sit, stay, stand, chase when requested. Most important the dog should be having fun.

Ratings for Barking Hills:

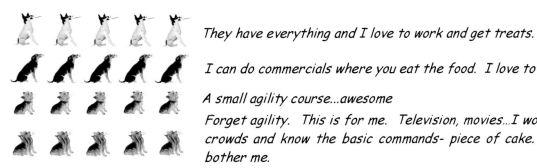

They have everything and I love to work and get treats.

I can do commercials where you eat the food. I love to be the center of attention!

A small agility course...awesome
Forget agility. This is for me. Television, movies...I would be terrific. You need to be cute and go into crowds and know the basic commands- piece of cake. Going into Times Square at midnight wouldn't bother me.

Sexy Beast

Pawdicures, Swedish massage, sports massage, whirlpool baths, hydrotherapy; certainly the world is going to the dogs! Hotels that cater to dogs often offer spa services, as do high-end doggie day care and grooming facilities.

We named this section after a new line of canine fragrance and finishing products that we wanted to share called SEXY BEAST...canine style unleashed. Check them out online at sexybeaststyle.com. They make a unisex eau de parfum and a three step system designed to use between groomings or baths that will cause "passing dogs to go weak in the knees". All kidding aside, Aspen, Vail, Mazel and Zoë visited their traveling grooming spa and all enjoyed it and came out smelling just great!

The philosophy at Sexy Beast is that when the love of your life is looking a bit shabby and smelling a bit off, it's time for their product, which is easy to use. All their products are "100% vegan, 100% safe and 100% sexy!

Ratings for Sexy Beast:

Nice! Not as aromatic as poop, but my people really liked getting close to me afterward.

Very nice! I just love a brushing and a snuggle.

I didn't like the messing with my puppy cut.

I needed my hair brushed and shaped.

Trendy Dogs

Trendy dogs are the new fashion statement. Designers of fame and fortune outfit the dogs; there are Hermes leads and collars, Gucci's, little black coat (serving the same well dresses purpose as the little black dress?) and Barney's cashmere sweaters and other luxurious items by Ralph Lauren. There are perfume sprays called" Oh My Dog', baskets and cosmetics by Vinton and Boyard and even a fashionable website www. Doggeneration .com

Grooming establishments have morphed into luxurious spas such as the Ritsy Canine and Doggie Doo and Pussycats Too in New York City. The Ritsy Canine has European Chrystal Chandeliers as part of the décor and offers massages combining Keike and acupuncture. For an overnight stay, the Spa offers private suites, room service and spa meals. At Doggie Doo and Pussycats too, the owners' dogs Trevor and Jessica are the doggie hosts and there is a full complement of natural botanical products used for grooming.

Spas are increasingly popular throughout the country and are often part of Pet resorts. For example, The Los Angeles Dog works offers hydrotherapy, massage, day care, grooming training and cage free boarding. The Chateau Marmutt also offers grooming, massage and designer beds. Philadelphia, the city of brotherly love, loves dogs too and canines can indulge at Mazzu Canine and Feline Hotel, sleep on platform beds, be provided 40 minute walks to the dog park and be cared for 24/7. Doggie Indulgence in Willow Grove New Jersey has a swimming pool for relaxation and therapy, as does the Applewood Pet Resort in Paradise Valley Arizona

Ratings for trendy spas etc.

 *Come on Mom.. this stuff is for you, not me…. right.*

 Ditto

 What do they think I am. a sissy? But, maybe I'll try the hydrotherapy.

 Now, this my element! It will make me more beautiful, inside and out.

We visited some local spa /grooming /day care establishments, but our dogs were unable to give these any positive barks. Our advice is to look carefully beyond the promotion and try to evaluate what the experience will be like for your dog.

Aspen and Vail give 5 barks to "Home Away From Home" pet sitting in Monroe, NY, where they were integrated into the family of people and dogs, slept on the beds and sofas, ate home cooked meals and got lots of loving attention. Check out the photos at http://www.flickr.com/photos/homeawayfromhome/ or contact ettie@optonline.net The owner offers pick up and delivery in Bergen County and beyond, which can include Hoboken and NYC. Belly rubs, ball play and supervised play are all included- no extra charge! If you believe your dog will do better in a home environment than a more commercial setting, you can start by asking veterinarians or rescue shelters in your area for recommendations.

Take Your Dog to Work

All through human history, dogs have worked alongside humans. They made themselves indispensable using their extraordinary senses as hunters, ratters, protectors and companions of the lonely shepherd in the area of first domestication of plants and animals - the Middle East. Sometimes, as in Egypt and Mesopotamia, they were venerated as Gods and in other periods they accompanied their masters to war as humans fought to conquer territories and other peoples.

Today, dogs are less needed for work and more for their unconditional affection for their human companions. Studies indicate that employees are more productive and less subject to stress when a dog brightens their day. Whether it is in a store, real estate office, bank or corporate offices, dogs find their place.

There are companion dogs, rescue dogs, and dogs who are welcomed at Internet giants such as Google and Amazon. The American Humane Association has done studies that indicate that businesses that allow dogs show an increase in staff morale and worker productivity. Interestingly there is also greater camaraderie and an increase in sales.

This year will be the seventh Take Your Dog to Work program and 10,000 companies are participating. The Boston Globe reported similar findings of lowered stress and a lift in morale. Employees are genuinely burned out if their canine does not show up for work. The owner of the eyeglass store, Optika, remarked that her dog, Sally, had sold more product than she did. The Humane Society of Greater Miami has instituted a program that brings dogs and cats into workplaces to help employees feel better and to promote a new venue for adoption.

Certainly, the dogs need to be good canine citizens to be welcomed for the joy they bring. Their work is different today in a time when industrialization, globalization and a high tech society may dehumanize the work environment; so humans turn to the most compassionate creature of all - the family dog. Many individuals spend more hours in the business environment than in the family home, so it is no wonder that there is the desire to reproduce the comforts of home, including taking the dog to work.

Every Dog Lover Needs a Dog

Every dog lover needs a dog to truly enjoy the Good life! Literally thousands upon thousands of wonderful puppies, kittens, dogs and cats are available for adoption or rescue from shelters, animal control pounds and rescue groups. There are rescue groups for each pure breed if you must have one. Petfinder.com is a wonderful resource which enables people to go online, enter their location or breed preferences and find listings from rescue groups and shelters around the country. Adoption policies vary from one group to another, so be persistent to find a good match.

Many people are under the misconception that rescued dogs have "problems". Dogs arrive in shelters for a variety or reasons. Sometimes the pet's guardian has died and no arrangements were made for the pet's care. Some dogs are found wandering in the streets with no identification and are either lost or abandoned. A human's allergies may cause a dog to be put up for adoption. Sadly, many people will purchase or adopt a puppy and after a few months decide that a dog is too much trouble for them. Most dogs available for adoption are adorable, wonderful companions and have no more "problems" or "issues" than dogs in general. Every dog I have had has been a rescue and each one has been spectacular. They are affectionate, loyal, smart and well behaved. The more you invest in a relationship with your dog, the more you will get back. The ticket to having a great dog is not how much money you spend or the dog's pedigree, but whether the dog receives adequate training, exercise and social time.

My personal preference is for mixed breeds. Each mixed breed dog is unique and mixed breeds are often healthier than purebred dogs. One great advantage to going to a shelter or adopting an adult dog is that knowledgeable staff can tell you about the dog's personality, temperament and needs to help you find a good match for your home or family

Some people shy away from shelters because they think they will be too depressing. Quite the contrary, as a result of growing public awareness and the influence of organizations such as Maddie's Fund, today's shelters can be very pleasant facilities where you would enjoy visiting or volunteering. Many animal control shelters strive to become "no kill". Animal rescue groups also take dogs at risk from local animal control facilities to their no kill shelters. These are the fortunate dogs that will have a second chance for a forever home with committed staff and volunteers dedicated to that goal. Good rescue groups will spay/ neuter, vaccinate, give needed medical attention and even provide training and socialization opportunities when appropriate. For people who do not have the time, patience or knowledge to train a puppy, adoption enables them to bring home an adult dog that is already housebroken, through the chewing stage and often trained.